Travel Journal
Kauai

VPJournals

Copyright © 2015 VPJournals

All rights reserved.

ISBN-13: 978-1518844836
ISBN-10: 1518844839

CONTENTS

Hi, I hope you enjoy this journal. It is packed with cool stuff and recommendations for you trip to Kauai, and has plenty of space to record details of your trip.

What's Inside	Page
Before you go to Kauai	
Great places to visit in Kauai	6-7
Cool places to visit in Kauai with kids	8-9
Good places to eat	10-11
Research Kauai	12-13
Postcard & Packing List	14-19
Kauai facts	21-22
Helpful hints	23-26
Clothes and shoe sizing charts, to help you get the right sizes while there	
Kauai Trip Diary	27-111
21 day trip diary to record details of your trip	
Reflect on you Trip	
Summary of your trip	113-121
People you met	123-125
Useful Resources	127-136
Size conversion charts	129-132
Common Translations	133-134
Notes	135-136

Have fun in Kauai

Great Places to visit in Kauai

Na Pali Coast	✓
Waimea Canyon	
Kalalau Trail	
Kauai Path	
Hanakapiai Falls	
Polihale State Park	
Hanalei Beach	
Tunnels Beach	
Hanalei Bay	
Kilauea Point National Wildlife Refuge	
Ke'e Beach	
Kalapaki Beach	
Kauai Coffee Company	

Koke'e State Park	
Lumahai Beach	
Na Pali Makai	
Queen's Bath	
Salt Pond Beach Park	
Shipwreck Beach	
Ho'opi'i Falls	
Na Pali Sea Breeze	
St. Raphael Church	
Kealia Beach	
Puu Poa Beach	
Kauai's Hindu Monastery	
Kileaua Point National Wildife Refuge Lighthouse	
Halele'a Gallery	

Cool Places to visit in Kauai with Kids

Poipu Beach Park	✓
National Tropical Botanical Garden	
Limahuli Garden and Preserve	
Allerton Garden	
Waimea Canyon State Park	
Hideaways Beach	
Grove Farm Museum	
Lydgate State Park	
Hanapepe Friday Night Festival & Art Walk	
Anini Beach	
Wailua Falls	
Na Aina Kai Botanical Gardens	

Lawai Beach	
Lydgate Beach Park	
Kilohana Plantation Estate	
Pali Ke Kua Beach (Hideaway Beach)	
Kauapea Beach (Secret Beach)	
Smith's Tropical Paradise	
Kauai Museum	
Kalihiwai Beach	
Kekaha Beach Park	
Wailua River State Park	
Manawaiopuna Falls (Jurassic Park Falls)	
Kadavul Hindu Temple	
Prince Kuhio Park	

Good Places to Eat in Kauai

Beach House Restaurant	✓
Hukilau Lanai	
Brennecke's Beach Broiler	
Gaylord's at Kilohana	
Duke's Canoe Club	
Keoki's Paradise	
Red Salt	
Tidepools	
Plantation Gardens Restaurant	
Verde Restaurant	
The Mediterranean Gourmet	
Ono Family Restaurant and Shave Ice	

Kauai Grill	
The St. Regis Bar	
Puka Dog	
Living Foods Market	
Fish Express	
Da Crack	
Merriman's Poipu	
Bar Acuda	
Koloa Fish Market	
Roy's Poipu Bar & Grill	
Smith Family Garden Luau	
Bouchons	
Tortilla Republic Grill + Margarita Bar	

Best Websites to Research Further

Do some more research on the internet to plan your trip:

www.wikipedia.org/wiki/Kauai
www.gohawaii.com/en/Kauai
www.lonelyplanet.com/usa/hawaii/kauai
www.kauai.com
www.kauai.gov
www.travelsmarthawaii.com
www.Hawaii.com
www.govisithawaii.com
www.hawaiitourismauthority.org
www.hawaii-guide.com

More places I want to visit on our trip

1. _____
2. _____
3. _____
4. _____
5. _____
6. _____
7. _____
8. _____
9. _____
10. _____
11. _____
12. _____
13. _____
14. _____
15. _____

Postcard List

Name:

Address:

Name:

Address:

Name:

Address:

Name:

Address:

Name:

Address:

Name:

Address:

Name:

Address:

Name:
Address:

Name:
Address:

Name:
Address:

Name:
Address:

Name:
Address:

Name:
Address:

Name:
Address:

MAIL

Packing List

✓	This Journal		Toiletries
	Tickets		Water
	Passport		Watch
	Money		Snacks
	Chargers		Umbrella
	Batteries		Towel
	Book to read		Guide book
	Camera		Kindle
	Tablet		Jacket
	Sun glasses		Medication
	Sun cream		*Add more below*

Kauai Facts

- Kauai is geologically the oldest of the main Hawaiian Islands. It's origins are volcanic, the island having been formed by the passage of the Pacific plate over the Hawaii hotspot.

- A possible translation of Kaua'i is "place around the neck", meaning how a father would carry a favorite child. Another possible translation is "food season"

- The native name for Kaua'i was Taua'i, and the major settlement of Kapa'a would have been called Tapa'a

- Mount Waialeale on Kauai is one of the wettest place on earth. It has 460 inches of rain each year

- Kauai, also known as the 'Garden Isle' is famous for its jagged green mountains, white-sand beaches and tropical landscapes. More than 60 Hollywood movies have been filmed there, including Jurassic Park

- English and Hawaiian are official languages. English is the main language spoken in the Hawaiian Islands

- Kapaʻa, on the "Coconut Coast" (site of an old coconut plantation), is the largest town with a population of 10,700

- Princeville, on the island's north side, was once the capital of Kauaʻi

- Kauai's official island flower is the Mokihana (a green berry found in the forest used in lei making)

- Kauai has the only navigable rivers in the state and the longest river is the Wailua River at 19.2 miles

- Waimea Canyon, which is part of Waimea Canyon State Park is at 3,000 feet (914 m) deep. Waimea Canyon is often referred to as "The Grand Canyon of the Pacific"

- The Na Pali Coast is a center for recreation in a wild setting, including kayaking past the beaches, or hiking on the trail along the coastal cliffs. There is another headland, Kuahonu Point, on the south-east of the island.

- One of Captain Cook's earliest maps of the Kauaʻi put its name as Atoui, though that was soon abridged to Atooi by many new arrivals, until the Hawaiian language was standardized, and it became Kauai

- Kauai's highest mountain is Kawaikini Peak at 5,243 feet (1,598 m)

Clothes & Shoe Sizes

Children's Shoe Sizes

UK	EUROPE	US	Japan
4	20	4½ or 5	12 ½
4 ½	21	5 or 5½	13
5	21 or 22	5½ or 6	13 ½
5 ½	22	6	13½ or 14
6	23	6½ or 7	14 or 14½
6 ½	23 or 24	7 ½	14½ or 15
7	24	7½ or 8	15
7 ½	25	8 or 9	15 ½
8	25 or 26	8½ or 9	16
8 ½	26	9½	16 ½
9	27	9½ or 10	16 ½ or 17
10	28	10½ or 11	17 ½
10½ or 11	29	11½ or 12	18
11 ½	30	12½	18 or 18 ½
12	31	13	19 or 19 ½
12 ½	31	13 or 13½	19 ½ or 20
13	32	1	20
13 ½	32 ½	1 ½	20 ½
1	33	1½ or 2	21
2	34	2½ or 3	22

Children's Clothing Sizes

UK	EUROPE	US	Australia
12m	80cm	12-18m	12m
18m	80-86cm	18-24m	18m
24m	86-92cm	23-24m	2
2-3	92-98cm	2T	3
3-4	98-104cm	4T	4
3-5	104-110cm	5	5
5-6	110-116cm	6	6
6-7	116-122cm	6X-7	7
7-8	122-128cm	7 to 8	8
8-9	128-134cm	9 to 10	9
9-10	134-140cm	10	10
10-11	140-146cm	11	11
11-12	146-152cm	14	12

Women's Shoe Sizes

UK	EUROPE	US	Japan
3	35 ½	5	22 ½
3 ½	36	5 ½	23
4	37	6	23
4 ½	37 ½	6 ½	23 ½
5	38	7	24
5 ½	39	7 ½	24
6	39 ½	8	24 ½
6 ½	40	8 ½	25
7	41	9 ½	25 ½
7 ½	41 ½	10	26
8	42	10 ½	26 ½

Women's Clothes Sizes

UK	US	Japan	France / Spain	Germany	Kauai	Australia
6/8	6	7-9	36	34	40	8
10	8	9-11	38	36	42	10
12	10	11-13	40	38	44	12
14	12	13-15	42	39	46	14
16	14	15-17	44	40	48	16
18	16	17-19	46	42	50	18
20	18	19-21	48	44	52	20

Men's Shoe Sizes

UK	EUROPE	US	Japan
6	38 ½	6 ½	24 ½
6 ½	39	7	25
7	40	7 ½	25 ½
7 ½	41	8	26
8	42	8 ½	27 ½
8 ½	43	9	27 ½
9	43 ½	9 ½	28
9 ½	44	10	28 ½
10	44	10 ½	28 ½
10 ½	44 ½	11	29
11	45	12	29 ½

Men's Suit / Coat / Sweater Sizes

UK / US / Aus	EU / Japan	General
32	42	Small
34	44	Small
36	46	Small
38	48	Medium
40	50	Large
42	52	Large
44	54	Extra Large
46	56	Extra Large

Men's Pants / Trouser Sizes (Waist)

UK / US	Europe
32	81 cm
34	86 cm
36	91 cm
38	97 cm
40	102 cm
42	107 cm

We have included another copy of this at the back of the book, so you can find it quickly again when you are in Kauai

Kauai Trip Diary

Write a daily diary during your trip

Day 1

Date: _____   **Weather:** _____

Day 2

Date: _____   **Weather:** _____

Day 3

Date: _____   **Weather:** _____

Day 4

Date: _____ **Weather:** _____

Day 5

Tip! Send your postcards

Date: _____   **Weather:** _____

Day 6

Date: _____   Weather: _____

Day 7

Date: _____ **Weather:** _____

Day 8

Date: _____ **Weather:** _____

Day 9

Date: _____ Weather: _____

Day 10

Date: _____   **Weather:** _____

Day 11

Date: _____   **Weather:** _____

Day 12

Date: _____   **Weather:** _____

Day 13

Date: _____   **Weather:** _____

Day 14

Date: _____   **Weather:** _____

Day 15

Date: _____ Weather: _____

Day 16

Date: **Weather:**

Day 17

Date: _____ **Weather:** _____

Day 18

Date: _____   **Weather:** _____

Day 19

Date: **Weather:**

Day 20

Date: _____   **Weather:** _____

Day 21

Date: _____   Weather: _____

Memories of your Trip

Things I will remember from the trip

Favorite Places visited on the Trip

People I Met

Name:
Address:
Tel:
email:

Name:
Address:
Tel:
email:

Name:
Address:
Tel:
email:

Name:
Address:
Tel:
email:

Name:
Address:
Tel:
email:

Name:
Address:
Tel:
email:

Name:
Address:
Tel:
email:

Name:
Address:
Tel:
email:

Name:
Address:
Tel:
email:

Name:
Address:
Tel:
email:

Name:
Address:
Tel:
email:

We hope you enjoyed your trip to Kauai

Please leave us a review if you found this Journal useful

Check out our useful resources on the next few pages

Clothes & Shoe Sizes

Children's Shoe Sizes

UK	EUROPE	US	Japan
4	20	4½ or 5	12 ½
4 ½	21	5 or 5½	13
5	21 or 22	5½ or 6	13 ½
5 ½	22	6	13½ or 14
6	23	6½ or 7	14 or 14½
6 ½	23 or 24	7 ½	14½ or 15
7	24	7½ or 8	15
7 ½	25	8 or 9	15 ½
8	25 or 26	8½ or 9	16
8 ½	26	9½	16 ½
9	27	9½ or 10	16 ½ or 17
10	28	10½ or 11	17 ½
10½ or 11	29	11½ or 12	18
11 ½	30	12½	18 or 18 ½
12	31	13	19 or 19 ½
12 ½	31	13 or 13½	19 ½ or 20
13	32	1	20
13 ½	32 ½	1 ½	20 ½
1	33	1½ or 2	21
2	34	2½ or 3	22

Children's Clothing Sizes

UK	EUROPE	US	Australia
12m	80cm	12-18m	12m
18m	80-86cm	18-24m	18m
24m	86-92cm	23-24m	2
2-3	92-98cm	2T	3
3-4	98-104cm	4T	4
3-5	104-110cm	5	5
5-6	110-116cm	6	6
6-7	116-122cm	6X-7	7
7-8	122-128cm	7 to 8	8
8-9	128-134cm	9 to 10	9
9-10	134-140cm	10	10
10-11	140-146cm	11	11
11-12	146-152cm	14	12

Women's Shoe Sizes

UK	EUROPE	US	Japan
3	35 ½	5	22 ½
3 ½	36	5 ½	23
4	37	6	23
4 ½	37 ½	6 ½	23 ½
5	38	7	24
5 ½	39	7 ½	24
6	39 ½	8	24 ½
6 ½	40	8 ½	25
7	41	9 ½	25 ½
7 ½	41 ½	10	26
8	42	10 ½	26 ½

Women's Clothes Sizes

UK	US	Japan	France / Spain	Germany	Kauai	Australia
6/8	6	7-9	36	34	40	8
10	8	9-11	38	36	42	10
12	10	11-13	40	38	44	12
14	12	13-15	42	39	46	14
16	14	15-17	44	40	48	16
18	16	17-19	46	42	50	18
20	18	19-21	48	44	52	20

Men's Shoe Sizes

UK	EUROPE	US	Japan
6	38 ½	6 ½	24 ½
6 ½	39	7	25
7	40	7 ½	25 ½
7 ½	41	8	26
8	42	8 ½	27 ½
8 ½	43	9	27 ½
9	43 ½	9 ½	28
9 ½	44	10	28 ½
10	44	10 ½	28 ½
10 ½	44 ½	11	29
11	45	12	29 ½

Men's Suit / Coat / Sweater Sizes

UK / US / Aus	EU / Japan	General
32	42	Small
34	44	Small
36	46	Small
38	48	Medium
40	50	Large
42	52	Large
44	54	Extra Large
46	56	Extra Large

Men's Pants / Trouser Sizes (Waist)

UK / US	Europe
32	81 cm
34	86 cm
36	91 cm
38	97 cm
40	102 cm
42	107 cm

Common Translations

English	French	Spanish	Italian
Hello	Bonjour	Hola	Ciao
Goodbye	Au revoir	Adiós	Arrivederci
Yes	Oui	Sí	Si
No	Non	No	No
Please	S'il-vous-plaît	Por favor	Per favore
Thank you	Merci	Gracias	Grazie
Excuse me	Excusez-moi	Perdón	Mi scusi
How much	Combien	Cuánto	Quanto
My name is	Mon nom est	Mi nombre es	Io mi chiamo
Where is	Où est	Dónde está	Dov'è
The bank	La banque	El banco	La banca
The toilet	Les toilettes	El baño	Il bagno

German	Japanese	Mandarin	Hindi
Hallo	Kon'nichiwa	Ni hao	Namaste
Auf Wiedersehen	Sayonara	Zaijian	Alavida
Ja	Hai	Shi de	Ham
Nein	Ie	Meiyou	Nahim
Bitte	Onegaishimasu	Qing	Krpaya
Vielen Dank	Arigato	Xiexie	Dhan'yavada
Entschuldigung	Sumimasen	Duoshao	Mujhe mapha karem
Wie viel	Ikura	Wo de mingzi shi	Kitana
Mein Name ist	Watashinonamaeha	Nali	Mera nama hai
Wo ist	Doko ni aru	Yinhang	Kaham hai
Die Bank	Ginko	Yinhang	Bainka
Die Toilette	Toire	Cesuo	Saucalaya

Notes:

Made in the USA
Middletown, DE
09 December 2018